First published in Great Britain in 1998 by Macdonald Young Books

This paperback edition published in 2002
by Hodder Wayland, an imprint of
Hodder Children's Books
a division of Hodder Headline Limited
338 Euston Road, London NW1 3BH

Designer: Kate Buxton
Language consultant: Betty Root
Consultant: Kate Wilcox, Relate

A CIP catalogue for this book is available from the British Library

Printed and bound in Grafiasa, Porto, Portugal.

ISBN 0 7500 2572 7

My Family's Changing

A FIRST LOOK AT FAMILY BREAK-UP

PAT THOMAS
ILLUSTRATED BY LESLEY HARKER

an imprint of Hodder Children's books

Something is happening in your family.
It is called divorce and you are all
going through it together.

Divorce is when
two people decide not
to be married to each
other anymore.

It is not your fault when your
parents get divorced, even
though it may feel like it.

When your mum and dad first met, they loved each other very much. They loved each other so much that they made a baby together.

And that baby was you.

Your parents may have hoped
that they would live together for
ever. But slowly, the way they felt
about each other changed.

The way your parents behaved towards each other changed too. You may have noticed them doing things like shouting at each other, or not talking at all.

This is how people behave when they are very unhappy.

When married people are this unhappy
they often choose not to live together anymore.

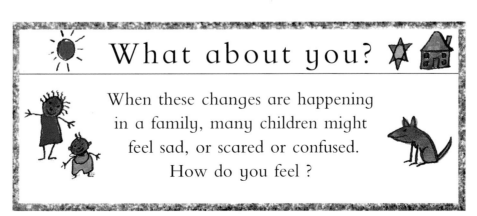

What about you?

When these changes are happening
in a family, many children might
feel sad, or scared or confused.
How do you feel?

Divorce can be upsetting for the whole family, so most parents only divorce after they have tried very hard to stay together.

You may worry that when your parents stop loving each other they will stop loving you too, but this will not happen.

You may also wish that your parents would get back together again, but this does not happen often – divorce is usually forever.

Before parents get divorced, they try to decide together
about things like where they will live
and where you will live.

When parents cannot agree about this, people
called solicitors and judges have to decide for them.
Sometimes it can take a long time to sort things out.

You may really miss the parent you are not living with. You may want to know what they are doing and when you can see them again.

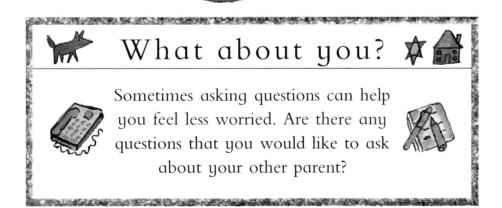

What about you?

Sometimes asking questions can help you feel less worried. Are there any questions that you would like to ask about your other parent?

Some children have overnight visits with one parent.
Others have special days when they can be with that parent.

Sometimes the other parent lives far away, but you can keep in touch with them by phone or by sending letters.

Doing things this way can feel strange at first, for all of you. It can take a while to find a way that works for everyone.

Your parents may seem different when they are away from each other. Sometimes they are happier than before, sometimes they are sadder.

Often the parent you are living with seems a lot busier, because with only one grown-up in the house there is more work to do. You can help by picking up clothes and toys.

Sometimes you may feel left out. Although divorce is something which happens to grown-ups, your feelings are important too. It is all right to ask questions if you want to.

What about you?

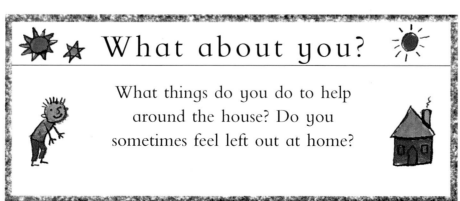

What things do you do to help around the house? Do you sometimes feel left out at home?

Spending time with other members of your family
and your friends can help you to feel better.
Talking to them, or to your teacher, about how
you feel may be easier than talking to your parents.

Sometimes you may feel so sad
or angry that it can be
hard to talk about
it to anyone.

But it is still
important to try. Otherwise, feelings
can build up inside you, like the air inside
a balloon, until you think you are going to pop.

It can be upsetting to think that now your family does not seem to be like your friends' families or those you often see on the television.

As you get older, you will begin to see that there are lots of different kinds of families. Although your parents are divorced, they are both still a part of your family.

At first you might feel that you have to choose between your parents. But you can go on loving both of them.

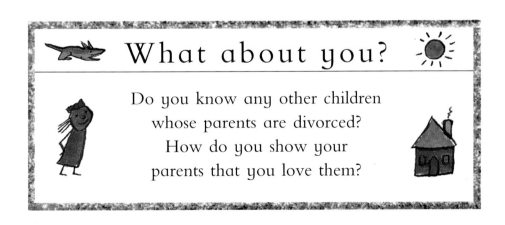

What about you?

Do you know any other children whose parents are divorced? How do you show your parents that you love them?

Sometimes parents say bad things about the other parent or buy lots of presents to make you love them more.

You may want to tell them not to do this and remind them that you enjoy being with each of them.

Sometimes you may feel upset or angry and push one of your parents away. You might do something naughty because you want to be noticed.

Your parents may tell you not to do this.

Divorce is painful for the whole family.
Each of you will have to learn
to do some things differently.

Everyone makes mistakes at first.
It is all right to make mistakes,
but we can try to learn from them.

Many things will change after your
parents' divorce, but the one thing that
will not change is their love for you.

HOW TO USE THIS BOOK

It can take a long time to talk through all there is to say about a divorce
and this book is meant to be read *with* a child, more than once.
Try reading it through first and familiarizing yourself with its content before you begin.

Here are a few guidelines:

From time to time you will see questions within the text. These 'prompts' are meant to give parents, teachers and children a chance to stop and talk with each other and ask each other questions. Use the prompts when they feel 'right'. If a child does not know how to answer, don't force the issue. You can always return to it later.

There will be plenty of time later, when a child is older, to talk about the complex 'whys' of a divorce. Initially, the most important thing is to help the child understand what divorce is and how it will affect his or her life. A child will need lots of support as he or she comes to terms with their own feelings about unexpected and often unwelcome changes.

Even if your divorce is for urgent reasons – such as child or spousal abuse – try not to make the mistake of assuming a child feels the same way you do. Children are very loyal and instinctively feel a need for both parents around them – even if one or both are inadequate or abusive. Go slowly and try to emphasise the benefits of getting out of such a situation.

Divorce should not be a taboo subject in school. Often this is the only place where a child may get a sense that he or she is not alone in the experience of a family breakdown. This idea may form the basis of a useful project, such as making family trees in a collage of photographs, drawings and words, which includes absent or extended family members.

GLOSSARY

Divorce   the ending of a marriage by law

Feelings   we feel something through our senses, such as when we feel hot or cold. We also feel things through our emotions, such as when we feel happy or sad

Judge   an independent person who listens to both sides of a divorce case and decides what action should be taken

Marriage   when a man and a woman become husband and wife by law

Solicitor   someone who is specially trained to help parents sort out the legal details of a divorce

FURTHER READING

Helpful Hands: You Will Always Be My Dad
by Ann De Bode and Ryan Bro Ere
(Evans, 1997)

How Do I Feel About: My Parents' Divorce by Julia Cole
(Franklin Watts, 1997)

What Do We Think About? Family Break-up
by Karen Bryant-Mole
(Wayland Publishers, 1998)

Your Emotions: I Feel Angry by Brian Moses and Mike Gordon
(Wayland Publishers, 1993)

Your Emotions: I Feel Sad by Brian Moses and Mike Gordon
(Wayland Publishers, 1993)

Your Feelings: I'm Lonely by Brian Moses and Mike Gordon
(Wayland Publishers, 1993)

Your Feelings: I'm Worried by Brian Moses and Mike Gordon
(Wayland Publishers, 1993)

RESOURCES

Gingerbread
35 Wellington Street, London WC2E 7BN 0207 240 0952
Support for one-parent families of both sexes. They run local group activities and publish information leaflets.

National Stepfamily Association
72 Willesden Lane, London NW6 7TA 0207 372 0844
(admin) 0207 372 0846 (confidential telephone counselling)
Local groups meet regularly. They also publish leaflets and run courses on step-parenting.

Parentline
Westbury House, 57 Hart Road, Thundersley,
Essex SS7 3PD 01268 757007
Voluntary self-help organisation offering confidential support to parents under stress. Groups meet throughout the country.

Relate: Marriage Guidance
Herbert Gray Cottage, Little Church Street,
Rugby CV21 3AP 01788 573241
Marriage guidance and advice. Phone for details of local groups or look in the phone book under 'marriage guidance'.